VOICES

NOT YOUR AVERAGE TYPE

we are prisoners all,
chained to the machinery of time...
...each of us statistics,
to a universal crime.

If life were compared to a game of chess...
...what chance do I stand
when I've already lost my queen?

Lost for words

I'm lost, lost for words
Having so much to say and
No way to say it

Losing your life
Through debilitating illness
Makes me feel lost, lost for words

Being held down by six nurses
And injected with medication
Makes me feel lost, lost for words

Taking a brisk walk
Drugged up, depressed and isolated
Makes me feel lost, lost for words

Losing your selfish self
And coming back to life
Makes me feel lost, lost for words

Being held down by six nurses
and injected with medication
makes me feel lost, lost for words

Hoping that dream will be answered
And looking for a love that was once so real
Makes me feel lost, lost for words

Taking time to reflect on goals
And ambitions of the past
Makes me feel lost, lost for words

Gaining self-confidence and losing my inhibitions
Developing peace of mind
Makes me feel lost, lost for words

Learning to live in the moment
And forgiving myself for past unhappiness
makes me feel lost, lost for words

trap

This is no prayer
This is no joke
This is no play

On wards

8-11-07

To

Jan

I have been thinking about my contribution to the Not Your Average Type antholigy. As such I don't feel happy having Imagen He Said in the book ~~in its curre~~ in the form it is in. Sinse I wrote that I have made some amendments to the text, and made it a stronger poem. Also I feel that as it is, it would be verry hard for someone with poor eyesight to read. I am sugesting either I submit a typed up copy of the amended verson or I just have he was a poet in the book. I hope you can see my logic in what I am saying, I would be gratefall to discuss this.

All the best

Frank

Imagen a jar of olives he said
On a hot day in the meditarian sun
I imagened
but I had never been to the mediteranian
though I once knew someone who had.
I imagend
as nite fell
and I felt alone
I thought of you.
I sat here
by this nite light
I tried
to write you this letter
as much as my confidence would allow me.
~~Cast out~~ Lonely shaddows
trudging on the street
I hold your hand ~~in my dreams~~

Frank Bangay
June 07

Imagine he said

A jar of olives

On a hot day in the Mediterranean sun,

But I have never been to the Mediterranean

Though I once knew someone who had.

I imagined

Night fell

I felt alone

I thought of you.

I sat by a night light

I tried to write you a letter

As much as my confidence would allow me.

Lonely shadows

I am trudging the streets

I love you

I hold your hand.

I Cherish You I love you Im 30 I went to Texas & got ROSSES

Im 20 Im Working for £73 an hour Iam

God Made the FOOTIDGE of me & Now Your talking to Me Im 39 O.K

you just Sat There doing Me no Harm Im 9 Right You Gave me £3.20

bracket • *n.* **1** a support at-tached toand projecting from a vertical surface. **2** a shelf fixed with such a support to a wall. **3** each of a pair of marks ()[]{}<> used to enclose words or figures. **4** a group classified as containg similar elements or falling between given limits (*income bracket*). (**bracketed, bracketing**) **1** **a** couple (names etc.) with a bracket. **b** imply a connection or equality between. **2** **a** enclose in brackets as parenthetic or spurious. **b** *Math.* enclose in brackets as having specific relations to what precedes or follows. [from Spanish *bragueta* 'codpiece, bracket']

Depression

Take me to the highest mountain
and let me see if I can see the views

No it's just blank

Take me to the sea
where the waves turn my insides

No it's just blank

Take me to the dressiest clothes shop in town

No it's just blank

Take me to the countryside
where the grass is cut so even
and the flowers smell so delicately

No I just feel blank

Take me to the mountain again
when I am alive
take me to the seas
where I can dive
take me back to life again

and let me really see it

The End of the World.

The world is nearly over,
Was the murmur in the sea,
All the fish seemed to know,
As did all that lived underneath.

The word grew bigger as it
travelled.
Along the ocean floors.
But in response, much like our
world,
It did not open hopeful doors.

MKANUDOTI

Mkanudoti
Was the child of the earth
Came from the earth
And was the earth

She was told by mother earth
Never to touch water or
Wash in it

In the desert and times of drought
She survived, lived and flourished

Suddenly something disturbing
And frightening lingered in the air
Like an answer blowing in the wind
Hot air and cold air meeting in mild air
At the zenith of the hour

And they spit on each other
And it rains heavily to clear the air
And

Mkanudoti
The only child of the earth
Melts

tation of being Australia's
leading sporting city. It is the
home of Australian Rules
every September.
the CBD, created by Chinese
migrants who came to Mel-
bourne during the goldrush
Chui Chow restaurant.
some of
hotels.
Where to stay
Pick your hotel wisely, with
reference to the locations of
your meetings.
locations.
Emirates Towers is the
power option here. Those vis-
iting Jebel Ali or the "free
sophisticated mix.
is routinely voted
most livable

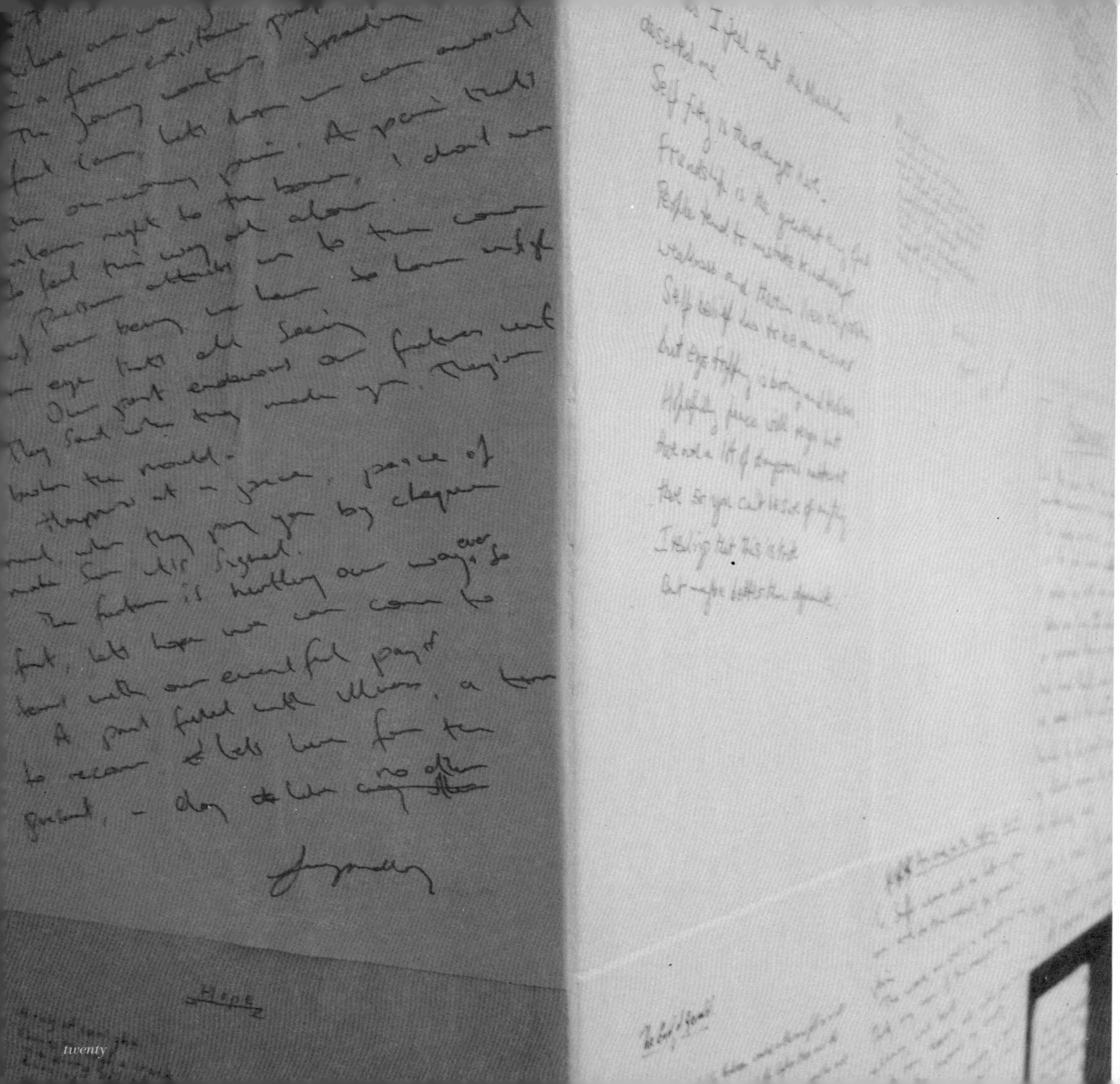
Hope
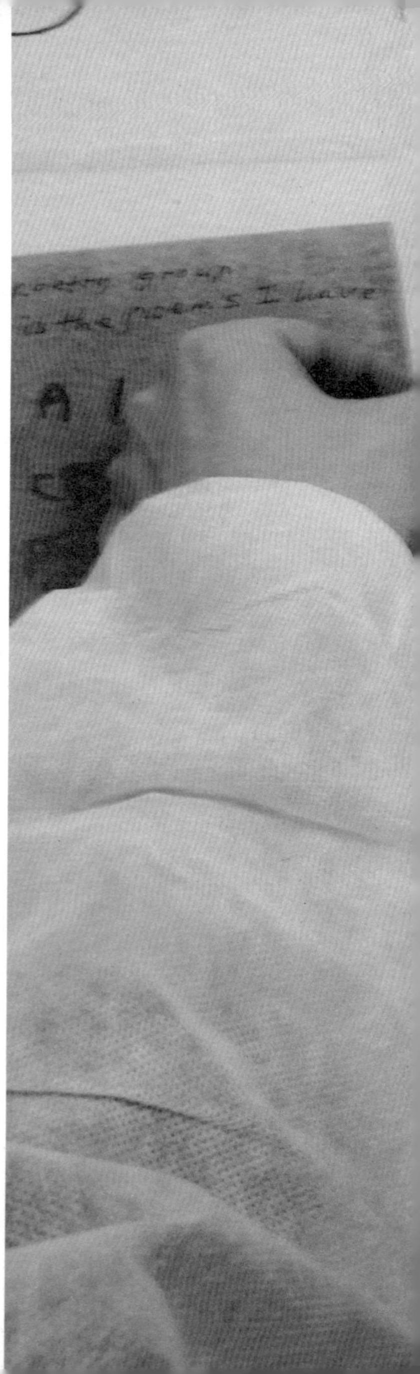
poetry group
the poems I have

SHAMBLES IS
ORDER

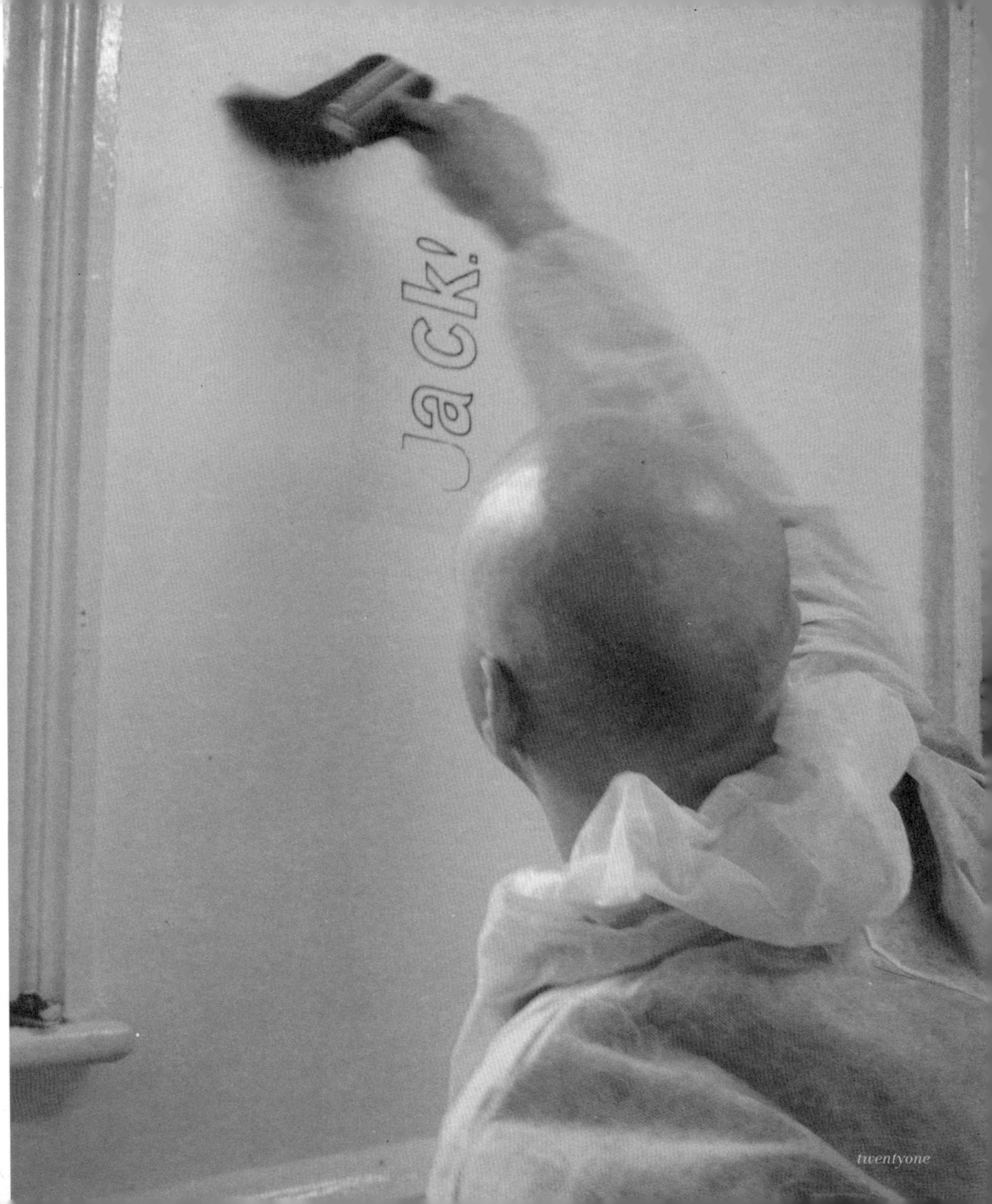
Jack!

THE END OF GERALD Gerald looked out of his bedroom window as the snow fell on a cold winter's morning. It held crisp against the leafless trees and the rocks that lined the path.

Feeling the cold noose around his neck, he kicked away at the chair and hung, twitching in the coolness of the room. Six months earlier...

Fragile
the needle point
blunt as it touches my skin
in voice gentle.
As metal touches wire slides.

Tone fluctuate in arms
Battery
As battle rages outside
Windows
The glass
footsteps
Round through Rain Split
Streets.

Sordid affairs.
Spell. black. magic.
Ink. Paper
As we discussed

traversing. the possibility.
left. Alone.

In the War Zone

Seems. impossible as

Hands. clutch Arms.
And the cold
Sets. in under blankets

Warm only when we next
meet.

PERRA

PERRO

PERROS
HACÍENDO
EL AMOR

PERRA
PERRITOS

PERROS

Core Dump

Fatal Error:

50 6C 65 61 73 6C 20
70 76 74 20
49 6F 75 72 20
72 75 62 62 69 73 68
69 6E 20
74 68 65 20
62 69 6E

Poetry is...

The song in my mind
The beat of my heart
The rhythm of my feet

Poetry is to see what you cant see
Or make clear what you can

Poetry can be found in anything
Yet it is free
Poetry is not just in your mind
Your mind can be in poetry

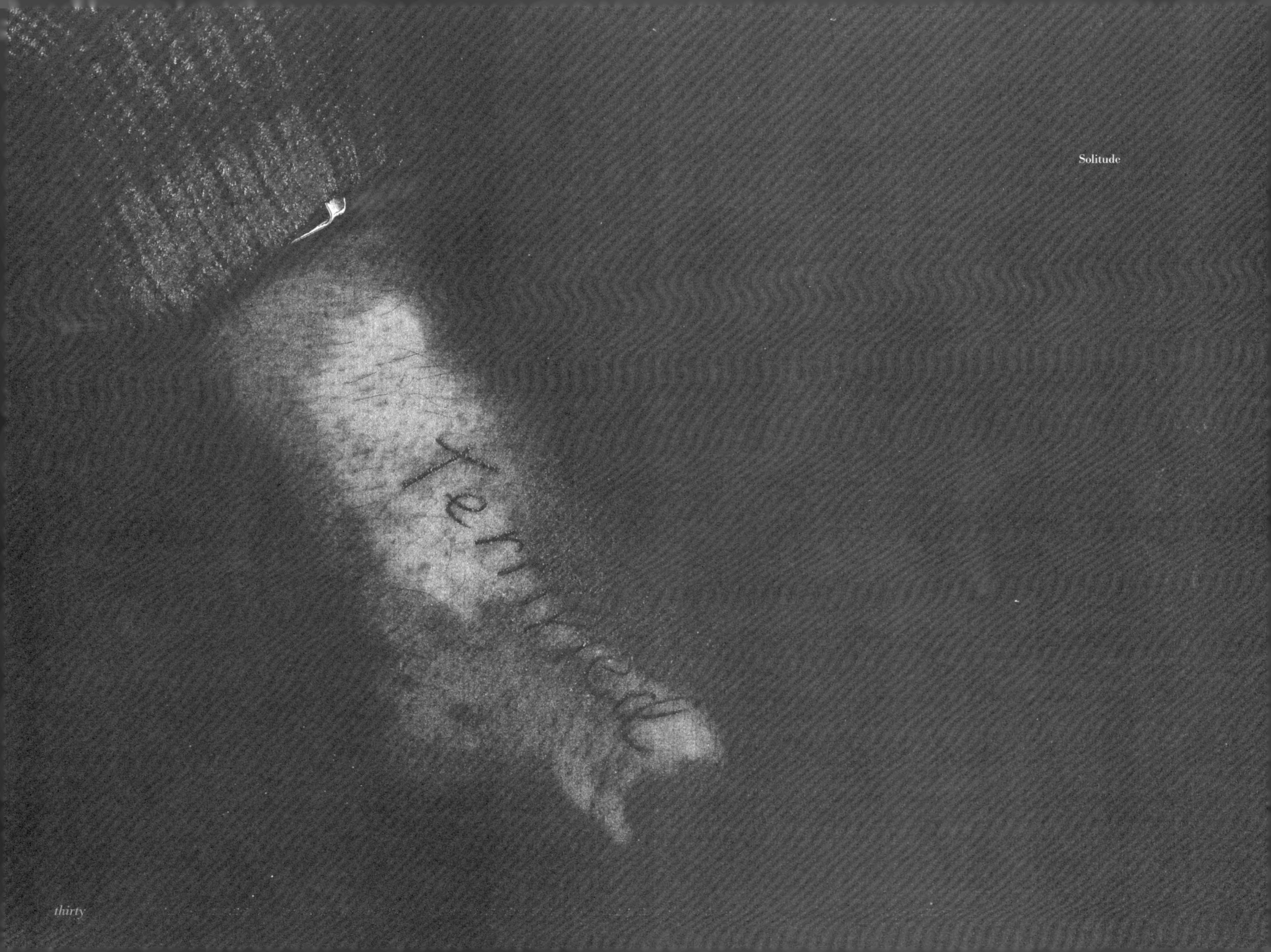
Terrified

I sat within the well clawed by my own hands
As the light behind my eyes flickered, soft to fade
Slowly I was blind
My fixed sterile smile melted into me
The chime of mankind swelled the air
But, I am safe here
Against the world, the desires I have hidden from
Now I belong to solitude and its me alone

Madness

1

I am nothing
But barking and black

2

Nothing is black
But all is barking

3

Barking, black, then
Nothing

4

The black dog
Barking then
Nothing

5

Nothing is barking
All is black

6

Nothing she said
Black barking

Give it back
Give it back
without it a big part of me
I lack I can't eat I
can't sleep but most of all
all i do is weep
Give it back give it back
because without it a Big
thirtythree

Come, ye Sons of Art:
Two Poems for Cultural Loitering

(I) The Poet Speaks

"You treat world history as a mathematician does mathematics, in which nothing but laws and formulae exist, no reality, no good and evil, no time, no yesterday, no tomorrow, nothing but an eternal shallow, mathematical present."

Otto Hess, on current economic theory

Who are your role models?
Oh, an eclectic bunch of relics
And hard to circumnavigate:
Sir Thomas Beecham (No, don't ask)
Groucho Marx, and Harpo.
John Stuart Mill and Dr Johnson.
Jonathan Swift, alongside Saki.
Hogarth, he's in there somewhere;
Shaw, Wells, Russell, a dash of Blake -
Quentin Crisp and Katherine Mansfield.
Bugs Bunny. Above all: Albert Steptoe.

Kindly give a thumbnail portrait of yourself.
A living fossil, susceptible to flattery.
A cynical and saturnine curmudgeon.
An ageing and eccentric bore.
A decrepit homunculus.
A tortoise steeped in a peat bog.
A polyp in the bowel of material production.
A senescent blatherer of overheard indiscretions.
A gadfly. A Grotesque (and not even Rococo).

Why do you carry on, churning out reams of nonsense?
Because I believe that consciousness is a curse. Because I believe you have to let me make the best of it.

You wasted your youth on philosophy and psychology. Why?
So as to arm me with a lifetime of vaguely ominous platitudes.

You have a certain superficial education. When did you resolve not to be an accountant, a financier?
Let me see. That would be...when I read the research, showing that economists thought the same way as people with an Antisocial Personality Disorder. "The ramifications of Game Theory", didn't you call it?

We noted your self-aggrandising glibness.
Mea culpa! If I'd spotted the gravy train younger, I could have made a flea-sized television pundit for our coffee-table classes.

A puddle of self-love being your defining characteristic: was there no place for you as a fashion designer? An Executive Producer? A celebrity? A sociologist?
Do you know: all of a sudden, I feel quite proud to stick just where I am.

(II) For Lauren

"I have to try and think what an artist is, beyond a hooligan who cannot live within his income of praise..."

Quentin Crisp

You say you want to meet again, but why?
Could you so much as see, above your foam of
ruthless private glamour?

Don't speak of "works of love".
Will you so much as hear my footfall - above the clamour
Of fathomless, stupefying vanity?

MY EGO
LOVES
ME

AUTOMATIC
(DOORS)

FAST
FOOD

CARS

LIFE

A 21st Century Picture
Now in this 21st Century
the picture unfolds before
me Fast food automatic
doors now paint the land
Cars and cars and more
cars pound the roads Car
horns and road rage
scream deadlines to the
air On the streets the car
is king Now rulers of
the landscape Mobile
phones and information
technology Now the art of
conversation Still the
birds keep singing Still
flowers embrace the soil
Time Time Time

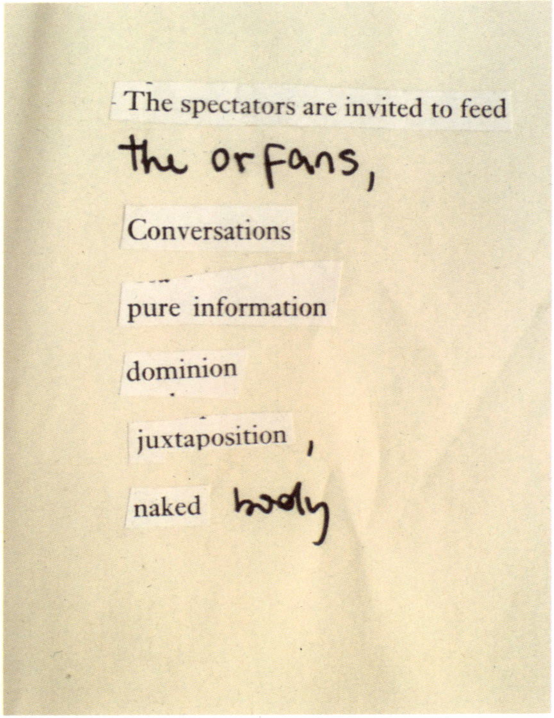
The spectators are invited to feed
the organs,
Conversations
pure information
dominion
juxtaposition ,
naked body

- the kidnapper's story

I hear

I hear voices

I hear voices in my head

I hear voices in my head sometimes

I hear voices in my head sometimes I understand

I hear voices in my head sometimes I understand what they are saying

I hear voices in my head sometimes I understand what they are saying to me

I hear voices in my head sometimes I understand what they are saying to me sometimes

I hear voices in my head sometimes I understand what they are saying to me sometimes I don't

I hear voices in my head sometimes I understand what they are saying to me sometimes I don't hear voices

A cold day in July
in the unbearable heat
of a factory where noise
drowned hungry men.

On a mountain-top a philosopher
found a stream,
and walked it
as a thousand waking figures slept
through an avalanche that never arrived.

A dog whined
and dined - trapped and free
as a cloud on
the broken horizon.

A figure
alone by a path
felt the humdrum hand of the multitude and,
his purpose ill-defined,
found meaning
where there was nothing else.

Because you want a third.

Pebbles pink, whitey grey speckled, smoothed out by centuries of seawater, tumble, rise and fall as if trying to reach the surface for air. Futile gesture, for this is an enclosed flimsy world with it's own momentum and rhythms. Starfish flit deftly between fronds of purple and brown seaweed, sometimes in pairs, their points raised up in unison as if they were dancing the can-can.

Silver lies on his back, his eyes staring upwards. It was not always like this. He had enjoyed many adventures and liasons with his sea neighbours, cutting a dashing figure in his turquoise catsuit, studded with crystalline jewels. Silver loved to dance and was renowned for his belly dancing, holding court for his many fans who, keen to learn his art, queued at his cave all night to await instruction from the maestro.

Silver spent his days twirling and whirling, making the movements appear easy and uncontrived, slipping upwards, downwards as only a truly pliable, versatile, sea god could. He had a reputation to maintain, and if he wanted to keep his name as the coolest silver seahorse he just had to remain lithe and fit.

Of course, those delectable fronds of purple, green and translucent brown which waved so tantalisingly at him daily, helped. One or two flickers of his tongue and the gourmet morsels were consumed with gusto. In the sea world, seahorses were highly prized. Silver knew he had rarity value and remained determined to preserve his privileged position. Clearly, this superstar of the waves had special requirements which could only be provided by the nutrient rich food of the deep. The superfood helped keep Silver in shape and some whispered, was the secret of his truly extraordinary zest for life and continuous energy.

It was true that Silver never fell ill, like some of the other creatures that lived beneath the waves. Perhaps it was due to his naturally sunny disposition, his optimistic outlook. He just never succumbed to low spirits, which would occasionally afflict the other creatures, in particular, the crabs.

£20

You put Down

Hunch

Back

Hunchback, bunch back, lunch back

Crunch back, munch back, punch back

Staunch back

That's all right Jack

Potato stack, night back, left back

Instep, outstep

Out reach in beach

Mistress, distress, impress, emporess

Romany, inventory, laboratory, lavatory

Inbed, unbred, incest, instead of ancestral

Incestoral

Later today, maybe tomorrow Jack

£5 Pocket Money

He Was A Poet

He was a poet

But he wore an unfashionable raincoat
He was a mystic but the grey weather blocked his view,
He was English through and through
He believed in the old traditions
He longed for them to return
He dreamed of pie and mash shops
Reappearing on the high street.

He was a poet

He wrote loads of words
He was a philosopher
He longed to be heard,
He sat in Lyons Tea Houses
Over a cup of tea and a buttered scone
He would express his views
To anyone who would listen.

He is a poet

Some think he's funny in the head
He walks down the high street with his carrier bags,
He talks to himself
Sometimes he finds communication hard
But he believes that one day
The world will hear his words.

£27
GOOD

The new Year

I Sigh of relief

~~He~~ I see The mind in my eye.
and think about, it twice. it not
That far of now. I sigh. ~~blow~~ The surprise.
has a knife. The surgery.
mind. I wonder to cut open The
I wonder whether. its worth. it.
I Sigh of ~~relief~~ relief. it a matter
of time. before The end comes. I sigh.

Schopenhauer's Poodle

I trot along in front of Schopenhauer
the man whom sadness stalks
the man whom unhappiness hunts
I jog on along in front of Schopenhauer
in my short clipped coat.

Make this clear:
I am not a toy
I am a dog.
Make this clear also:
I am not a toy dog.
There are differences:
One: A toy dog can wag its tail
but it can never be happy
Two: You can never put a toy dog down

It is not a dog's job to question.
Every dog has its duty
the philosopher his destiny
my deity: obedience

Yes yes yes yes yes yes yes
I pant in my best dog's yesterday breath
trotting along in front of Schopenhauer
in search of his favorite Frankfurt sausage shops

(Schopenhauer loves sausage shops
sadly he dislikes sausages
Schopenhauer is suspicious of sausages
the origin of sausages horrifies him)

I am a simple pooch
and for me philosophy
is as simple as a sausage:
it is best not to watch it being made
best if you don't know
what has gone into it.

Such stuff and wad I leave up to him.
That I leave to the man I leave behind
the man hounded by unhappiness
dogged by sadness
the man daily at my tail.

But my arse hole shows no emotion
a constant o in front of his nose
a black zero, a dark star that he follows...

The only question I have I ask myself.
Do dogs have morals?
I can only think it is impossible
for dogs to think
about the wrong things.

The only question I have I ask myself.
A dog maybe man's best friend
but a man is not always
a dog's best friend

Elephants Don't Do Ballet Classes

Ballet classes tend to be for the upper classes
And elephants don't really fit in
As well as the others
Not like their eloquent brothers

The ballet shoes are too small for their big feet
To put them on is a real defeat
Their bodies cant do the step as one would like
Coz they're elephants...RIGHT?!

SEEDATED

£500
DLA 96
SF

DATED

you can always tell a Psychiatrist by his shoes.

April 25th 2000 came round sooner than what I expected.

Dr:[redacted] Psychiatrist
[redacted] : Social Worker
J MacDoughall: Customer

Approaching room 17 at the Host Centre 2:30.

"How punctual we are"
After finding out Mr Z[redacted] past family history and musing over his Grandfather who was in The Luftwaffe. We proceed. He's bending again. Sorry falling builds. Test Department and ur "What psychiatrick texts books do you get off on in your spare time?"

SO CRASS SO CRASS SO CRASS SO CRASS SO CRASS SO CRASS SO
CRASS SO CRASS SO CRASS SO CRASS SO CRASS SO CRASS SO CRASS
SO CRASS SO CRASS SO CRASS SO CRASS SO CRASS SO CRASS SO
CRASS SO CRASS SO LEBENSBORNE
AGAIN. four

“another doctor with a long nose and hairy arms walked up to put in his 2 cents”

no its small it's a fence no it's a wall its covered no its blank its floating no it sank its bitter not its sweet its tidy no its neat its round no its square i
no its bare its ugly no its pretty its rhyming no its slang its good no its bad its happy no its sad it's a breeze not it's a draught it's a whole no it's a halfi
o its full its open no its shut its tend no its tough its smooth no its rough Its large no its small it's a fence no it's a wall its covered no its blank its floatir
k its bitter not its sweet its tidy no its neat its round no its square its dressed no its bare its ugly no its pretty its rhyming no its slang its good no i
appy no its sad it's a breeze not it's a draught it's a whole no it's a halfits empty no its full its open no its shut its tend no its tough its smooth no i
s large no its small it's a fence no it's a wall its covered no its blank its floating no it sank its bitter not its sweet its tidy no its neat its round no its squar
ed no its bare its ugly no its pretty its rhyming no its slang its good no its bad its happy no its sad it's a breeze not it's a draught it's a whole no it's
mpty no its full its open no its shut its tend no its tough its smooth no its rough Its large no its small it's a fence no it's a wall its covered no its blan
ing no it sank its bitter not its sweet its tidy no its neat its round no its square its dressed no its bare its ugly no its pretty its rhyming no its slang i
its bad its happy no its sad it's a breeze not it's a draught it's a whole no it's a halfits empty no its full its open no its shut its tend no its tough its smoot
ugh Its large no its small it's a fence no it's a wall its covered no its blank its floating no it sank its bitter not its sweet its tidy no its neat its round n
e its dressed no its bare its ugly no its pretty its rhyming no its slang its good no its bad its happy no its sad it's a breeze not it's a draught it's a who
halfits empty no its full its open no its shut its tend no its tough its smooth no its rough Its large no its small it's a fence no it's a wall its covered no i
floating no it sank its bitter not its sweet its tidy no its neat its round no its square its dressed no its bare its ugly no its pretty its rhyming no its slan
no its bad its happy no its sad it's a breeze not it's a draught it's a whole no it's a halfits empty no its full its open no its shut its tend no its tough i
no its rough Its large no its small it's a fence no it's a wall its covered no its blank its floating no it sank its bitter not its sweet its tidy no its neat i
o its square its dressed no its bare its ugly no its pretty its rhyming no its slang its good no its bad its happy no its sad it's a breeze not it's a draught it
no it's a halfits empty no its full its open no its shut its tend no its tough its smooth no its rough Its large no its small it's a fence no it's a wall its covere
ank its floating no it sank its bitter not its sweet its tidy no its neat its round no its square its dressed no its bare its ugly no its pretty its rhyming n
its good no its bad its happy no its sad it's a breeze not it's a draught it's a whole no it's a halfits empty no its full its open no its shut its tend no i
s smooth no its rough Its large no its small it's a fence no it's a wall its covered no its blank its floating no it sank its bitter not its sweet its tidy no i
round no its square its dressed no its bare its ugly no its pretty its rhyming no its slang its good no its bad its happy no its sad it's a breeze not it's
it's a whole no it's a halfits empty no its full its open no its shut its tend no its tough its smooth no its rough Its large no its small it's a fence no it's
covered no its blank its floating no it sank its bitter not its sweet its tidy no its neat its round no its square its dressed no its bare its ugly no its prett
ing no its slang its good no its bad its happy no its sad it's a breeze not it's a draught it's a whole no it's a halfits empty no its full its open no its shu
no its tough its smooth no its rough Its large no its small it's a fence no it's a wall its covered no its blank its floating no it sank its bitter not its swee
o its neat its round no its square its dressed no its bare its ugly no its pretty its rhyming no its slang its good no its bad its happy no its sad it's a breez
draught it's a whole no it's a halfits empty no its full its open no its shut its tend no its tough its smooth no its rough Its large no its small it's a fenc
wall its covered no its blank its floating no it sank its bitter not its sweet its tidy no its neat its round no its square its dressed no its bare its ugly no i
s rhyming no its slang its good no its bad its happy no its sad it's a breeze not it's a draught it's a whole no it's a halfits empty no its full its open no i
tend no its tough its smooth no its rough Its large no its small it's a fence no it's a wall its covered no its blank its floating no it sank its bitter not i
tidy no its neat its round no its square its dressed no its bare its ugly no its pretty its rhyming no its slang its good no its bad its happy no its sad it's
ot it's a draught it's a whole no it's a halfits empty no its full its open no its shut its tend no its tough its smooth no its rough Its large no its small it
no it's a wall its covered no its blank its floating no it sank its bitter not its sweet its tidy no its neat its round no its square its dressed no its bare i
its pretty its rhyming no its slang its good no its bad its happy no its sad it's a breeze not it's a draught it's a whole no it's a halfits empty no its full i
its shut its tend no its tough its smooth no its rough Its large no its small it's a fence no it's a wall its covered no its blank its floating no it sank i
ot its sweet its tidy no its neat its round no its square its dressed no its bare its ugly no its pretty its rhyming no its slang its good no its bad its happ

465 03979734
COMPLETELY HYDRAULIC LTD
UNIT 3 VICTORIA PK IND
ROTHBURY RD
VICTORIA PK INDRI
LONDON
E9 5HD Rte: 03
1 items 3 kilo
FLOWTECH
KILOS
20285508
Killers
Reinventors
White Pill
sixtyfour

Crossing the Line

When I stepped over the edge
Did we lose our love?
When you saw me in bits
Did you lose your love for me?
When I fell I didn't think of you
How hard I was not to think of our love
I stepped over and you saw me torn

Voices one
by Angela Jack, Acrylic and mixed media on canvas

We Are Prisoners four
by Norman Caya

If Life Were A Game five
by Norman Caya

Lost for Words six
by Gary Molloy

Trap eight
by Dr W.S. Oddorgan. Acrylic on board

This Is No Prayer nine
by Angela Morris

Imagine A Jar Of Olives ten
poem and correspondence by Frank Bangay

Cynthia, Sonya, Martin and Stacey twelve
by Rudolph Lindo, felt tip pen on paper

Dictionary Definition fourteen
by Stuart Brown, pen and ink on paper

Depression fifteen
by Alison West

Video still from *A Face In Love* sixteen
by Alex Ingram

The End of The World seventeen
by Alex Ingram

Mkanudoti eighteen
by Odon Winkel

Untitled nineteen
by Jaemi Hardy, oil on board

The Poetry Room twenty
by Core Poets

The End of Gerald twentytwo
by Stephen Farrant

Fragile twentyfour
by Laura Allan

Perra, Perro, Perras twentysix
by Angela Jack, pencil on paper

Core Dump twentyeight
by Stephen Farrant

Poetry Is... twentynine
by Daniel Lewis

Terrified thirty
by Stan Champion

Solitude thirtyone
by Angela Rose

Madness thirtytwo
by Laura Allan

Give it Back thirtythree
by Unknown Artist

Two Poems for Cultural Loitering thirtyfour
by Stephen Jackson

My Ego Loves Me thirtyseven
by Jaime Valtierra, mixed media

Video stills and text from *A 20th Century Picture* thirtyeight
by Mary Wheelan

The Spectators Are Invited to Feed forty
by Unknown Artist

A Kidnappers Story fortyone
by Alex Ingram

I Hear Voices fortytwo
by Jan Noble

Because You Wanted a Third fortythree
by G.F

Short Story fortyfive
by Margret Drew

£20 You Put Down In The Bank fortysix
by Rudolph Lindo, felt tip pen on A4 paper

Hunch Back fortyseven
by Christopher Mulcahy

£5 pocket money fortyeight
by Rudolph Lindo, felt tip pen on A4 paper

He Was a Poet fortynine
by Frank Bangay

Good fifty
by Rudolph Lindo, felt tip pen on A4 paper

New Year fiftyone
by Simon Amoordon

Schopenhauer's Poodle fiftytwo
by Jan Noble

Diptych fiftyfour
by Jonathan Sheers, Acrylic on board

Elephants Don't Do Ballet Classes fiftysix
by Alison West

Police Call fiftyseven
by Laura Allan

Seedated fiftyeight
by Gary Molloy and Offshoot, Turf

You Can Always Tell A Psychiatrist sixty
photograph and notes by Jim McDougal

Piggy Teddy sixtytwo
by Marga Tormo-Moll, mixed media

Its Big from a poem sixtythree
by Una Thorpe

Selected Works sixtyfour
by Core Poets

Crossing The Line sixtyfive
by Anon

LOTTERY FUNDED

Hackney

core

Text a poem to Textism: 07903 548555. for more information go to www.myspace.com/nyatcore